Contemplations to

Grow By

A 90 Day Devotional To Challenge

You As You Cultivate Your

Relationship With Jesus

To my wife, Marika, and children, who motivate me to be a more godly man.

Acknowledgments

My congregation at Arise Alliance Church in Quartzsite, AZ. Thank you for your support in my ministry endeavors. And to Niki who helped bring this devotional to print.

Copyrighted Material

Scripture quotations marked (ESV) are from The ESV® Bible (The Holy Bible, English Standard Version®), © 2001 by Crossway, a publishing ministry of Good News Publishers. Used by permission. All rights reserved.

Scripture quotations marked (NIV) are taken from the Holy Bible, New International Version®, NIV®. Copyright © 1973, 1978, 1984, 2011 by Biblica, Inc.™ Used by permission of Zondervan. All rights reserved worldwide. www.zondervan.com. The "NIV" and "New International Version" are trademarks registered in the United States Patent and Trademark Office by Biblica, Inc.™

Scripture quotations marked (NLT) are taken from the Holy Bible, New Living Translation, copyright ©1996, 2004, 2015 by Tyndale House Foundation. Used by permission of Tyndale House Publishers, Carol Stream, Illinois 60188. All rights reserved.

A Note to the Reader

Dear Reader,

If you are reading this, then you picked up this book because your desire is my own, to be a more faithful disciple of our Savior. What you're about to read are thoughts on ninety verses from the Bible. My prayer and hope is that at the end of these ninety days, you will come out of it as a stronger disciple of Christ. If you take each day's thought seriously and challenge yourself to put these words into action, you will see a noticeable difference in your walk with the Lord. It's that difference that God has always intended for you and me. The Lord's purpose has always been to bring us out of sin and deeper into his holiness. In ninety days, I pray you'll experience that deeper holiness. Now, may you experience the great work of the Holy Spirit, who will accomplish the goal of the Father to conform you to the image of the Son. Amen.

In Christ's Grip,

Jeremiah

Therefore, there is now no condemnation for those who are in Christ Jesus, because through Christ Jesus the law of the Spirit who gives life has set you free from the law of sin and death.

Romans 8:1-2 (NIV)

THERE IS NO CONDEMNATION FOR THOSE WHO ARE IN CHRIST JESUS. So stop. Stop listening to that voice that says you're not good enough because Christ died for you. Stop listening to that voice that says God's not going to forgive you this time; he already has. Stop listening to that voice that says God is out to get you; he is constantly showing you that he is for you.

If you have put your trust into Jesus as your Savior, you are a new creation. You have been set free because the Son has set you free (John 8:36). Make it your mantra that you are free in Christ because of Christ, and he has no condemnation for you. Now, go live it.

Day 2

He has shown you, O mortal, what is good. And what does the Lord require of you? To act justly and to love mercy and to walk humbly with your God.

Micah 6:8 (NIV)

Why does Micah say, "you, O mortal…?" Why not "man," "human," "nations," etc.? Is it not because we are created by God? We are not divine; God is. We are not eternal; God is. We are merely created beings. And because of that, we do not make the rules. It is the Creator, the Divine, the Eternal One who does.

It is God who created us, and therefore, it is only God who can give us insight into purpose—a purpose that satisfies us, a purpose that makes this mortal life worth living, and a purpose that takes us into eternity.

We are mortal; God is not, and we must head in his direction if we desire to prosper. The question is, are we listening or rejecting?

Day 3

Wash and make yourselves clean. Take your evil deeds out of my sight; stop doing wrong. Learn to do right; seek justice. Defend the oppressed. Take up the cause of the fatherless; plead the case of the widow.

Isaiah 1:16-17 (NIV)

A changed life is in direct correlation with a right relationship with God. As we move deeper into relationship with God, God's desires become our own. As we grow in our understanding of God, his priorities become our own. As we engross ourselves into the transformational process that God is taking us through, we are illuminated to the world as God sees it.

And in this right relationship, our lives begin to shed all manner of evil. But if we are not willing to live in this right relationship, if we are not willing to shed all evil that is within us, if we are not willing to submit to God's cleansing, then we will not experience the full extent of the relationship that God saved us to.

Sure, we'll get glimpses and tastes, but never the fullness that we were saved to. Never the full meal of God's banquet. We will experience only scraps. But if we submit to God's working in our lives, if we seek to be cleansed of evil and to seek out justice, then we will experience our relationship with God in the way he has always intended us to.

Day 4

Therefore, with minds that are alert and fully sober, set your hope on the grace to be brought to you when Jesus Christ is revealed at his coming.

1 Peter 1:13 (NIV)

What does it mean to be alert and fully sober, and what is its connection to the coming of Jesus?

Does it not mean not allowing ourselves to be distracted by this world? Does it not mean that we are to understand this world's fate? Does it not mean that we are to engage our body and mind in a readiness that prepares itself for any moment Christ may return? Should we not then live our lives accordingly?

You and I are to be focused, not on this world and what we can gain from it. Not on its treasures and luxuries but on considering them all worthless compared to Christ.

You and I are to live this life in anticipation of Christ's return. That means we are not living in fear but rather in honest, humble, and godly lifestyles so that when Christ returns, we can stand before him ready. If Jesus would come today, would your life be something worth his return?

Day 5

But just as he who called you is holy, so be holy in all you do; for it is written: "Be holy, because I am holy."

1 Peter 1:15-16 (NIV)

Why should you and I take up the call to be holy? To be like God in removing ourselves from those things that are not in keeping with God's character? There are several reasons why. Obedience and love are the two most commonly referred to, but like those things, it goes back to the book of Genesis and the purpose of humanity.

You and I were created by a holy God to be holy people. We were not created to be in the state that we currently find ourselves in. We are fish on land, an electric eel with no spark, a sapling in an inferno.

We were created to be holy; it is our original state of being, and it is where we flourish. Today, do not think of being holy as God is holy as some impossible achievement, but rather getting back to the person that God originally created us to be. Back to who we are.

Day 6

When hard pressed, I cried to the Lord; he brought me into a spacious place. The Lord is with me; I will not be afraid. What can mere mortals do to me?

Psalm 118:5-6 (NIV)

God does not give up on us. No matter our circumstances, no matter what is assaulting us or what consequences of our actions are manifesting, God has not abandoned us.

If we cry out to him, if we seek a right relationship with him, God will meet us. He will break through the circumstances, through the assault, and through our consequences to bring hope and peace. He will bring us into an understanding and into the reality that all is in his hand, and nothing happens without his allowance.

God does not give up on us; we should never think he does, nor give up on him. Any other statement about this reality is a deception from things that are not of God.

Do you trust that he is there today? If you are in doubt, call and keep calling until you see it for yourself.

So in Christ Jesus you are all children of God through faith, for all of you who were baptized into Christ have clothed yourselves with Christ. There is neither Jew nor Gentile, neither slave nor free, nor is there male and female, for you are all one in Christ Jesus.

Galatians 3:26-28 (NIV)

In our day and age, everyone seems to be at war with everyone else: there's the war on women, racial wars, ideological wars, and so on. It looks like we will go to war over anything, if only to be correct.

But look at the example of God. He is the only one who is right. In all things, he is the only one who can pass judgment without impartiality. And yet, even though he is right and can make war with humanity, instead, he sends a mediator. However, it is not just any meditator who would make a treaty; he sends a mediator who dies to implement the treaty. To provide a way for reconciliation with God for anyone who would accept it.

In this treaty, all are welcome to participate. Our skin color and ethnicity make no difference, our gender makes no difference, and our social and economic status makes no difference. The treaty covers us all, and all can be reconciled on an equal level. The question is, do we want peace, or do we want war?

The choice is now ours because God has already made his.

Day 8

May the God who gives endurance and encouragement give you the same attitude of mind toward each other that Christ Jesus had, so that with one mind and one voice you may glorify the God and Father of our Lord Jesus Christ.

Romans 15:5-6 (NIV)

Have you ever connected endurance and encouragement to unity in the Church?

Do you know why I think they're connected? We're all sinners, and we get on each other's nerves sometimes. Because of that, we need God's strength to endure difficult people and situations. We all need the encouraging reminder that these people are not here randomly and that God has brought all of us into this body to build each other up.

Why do we need unity? Because through unity, the world will know that God is real and active.

So, when we encounter a difficult Christian, remember that God is the source we need to rely on to deal with them. When we rely on God, we can show that he is real in our lives and the Church.

Do everything without grumbling or arguing, so that you may become blameless and pure, "children of God without fault in a warped and crooked generation." Then you will shine among them like stars in the sky as you hold firmly to the word of life. And then I will be able to boast on the day of Christ that I did not run or labor in vain.

Philippians 2:14-16 (NIV)

Ever been rock climbing? I mean, real rock climbing. Not, oh, I'm going rock climbing, and you're just on a rock wall at an amusement park or where who gets on top of a couple of boulders and some rocks, you might slip on a beach. Actual rock climbing is on the side of a cliff, and you have to use ropes, and you have to find small slits in the rock to place your hands and feet in.

I'm talking about real rock climbing. In the Yosemite National Park in California, there is a peak called El Capitan. It is considered one of the most challenging peaks to rock climb because of its height and rugged sheer cliff. It stands 7,573 feet high. Recently, a pair of rock climbers scaled El Capitan; it took them 18 days to do it. All day, every day, they made their way up the cliff, sleeping and eating suspended in the air. One misstep, one false footing could have led to disaster. How long did it take for these rock climbers to believe themselves ready for a climb like this? Five years of training and countless other climbs to prepare them.

Just like the climbers who scaled El Capitan need to be precise in their steps to achieve the climb, Christians need to be precise in walking with the Holy Spirit to achieve the life God has for us. For Christians, missteps abound. It can feel like we take two steps and one back, slowly making our way into the life God has for us. We do this because we allow our desires, thoughts, and ambitions to lead us rather than walk in step with the Spirit.

I've been rock climbing once, nothing like El Capitan, but I learned something from it. It was easy to think a footing was secured, only to have that footing give way when I put my weight on it.

In the same way, it's easy to think our way is the best, only to have it fail us. Yet we are promised in the Bible that if we stay in step with the Spirit, he will keep our footing secured and our paths straight.

How do we do this? By placing ourselves in a position to get on the right path. We dive into God's word and change our minds and actions to fit it rather than trying to change it to accommodate us. When we do that, even El Capitan couldn't stop us.

Day 10

Brothers and sisters, if someone is caught in a sin, you who live by the Spirit should restore that person gently. But watch yourselves, or you also may be tempted.

Galatians 6:1 (NIV)

Restoration, not condemnation, should be the goal of every believer, whether it is a brother or sister who is struggling in their walk with God or a person who has never placed their trust in Jesus as their Savior. Restoration of the believer and nonbeliever to a right and growing relationship with God should be our desire.

Therefore, we must take steps to go before God to have our lives analyzed by the Spirit so that we are not found in the same sinful pitfalls that we are trying to steer others away from. Then, we can seek God to help us lovingly rebuke sinful actions and point people back to God.

Let us be like Jesus speaking to the woman caught in adultery, "Then neither do I condemn you…Go now and leave your life of sin." Let us be God's agents representing his restoration work.

Humble yourselves before the Lord, and he will lift you up in honor.

James 4:10 (NLT)

Humbleness isn't a lack of ability. Humbleness isn't the tearing down of our self-esteem or self-worth. Humbleness isn't trying to degrade ourselves for another's enjoyment. Humbleness is saying I will put others first and myself second. Humbleness is saying I will look to another's benefit before my own. Humbleness is saying I will not act for the good of myself but rather for the good of those around me. Humbleness thinks I will not let my pride control me; instead, I will overcome it.

Humbleness is realizing that our position in life is to pave the way for the God who saved us. To remove every barrier we've constructed in our lives, to allow our kingdom to be consumed by God's. Humbleness is realizing that we are to God, as an ant is to us, and then praising him for that greatness.

Only in humbleness can we know genuine appreciation and rise in true victory.

For we are not fighting against flesh-and-blood enemies, but against evil rulers and authorities of the unseen world, against mighty powers in this dark world, and against evil spirits in the heavenly places. Therefore, put on every piece of God's armor so you will be able to resist the enemy in the time of evil. Then after the battle you will still be standing firm.

Ephesians 6:12-13 (NLT)

Look around you. Do you see Christians being slaughtered on the news? It's happening. Do you see the lives that are being taken by drugs, alcohol, sex, and hopelessness? They're there. Do you see countries and societies bowing down under the pressure of an anti-Jesus movement? It's everywhere. Do you see that person who mocks you, bullies you and acts aggressively toward you? It's all connected. We may see the symptoms of battles when they spill over into the physical world, but the war rages not on the surface but behind the curtains of our hearts and minds.

We may see the destruction of lives with our physical eyes, but it's just a distraction from the real destruction that is happening within. God is fighting for the hearts and minds of the people; what is shown on the outside is just the repercussions of the war that wages in the unseen places of life.

We can complain about someone's symptoms and rage against their animosity and venom. But God has called us to do something great. He has called us to look past the surface symptoms and see the war that rages just beneath the surface. We are called to love those who hate us and pray for those who would be our enemies. When the war rages in us, the God of Heaven fights with ferocity and veracity.

As God's people, we are to realize that the battle is not against what we see but against what we don't see. We are to pray and intercede for those who are falling by the wayside to the enemy as he pushes them to spill his war out onto the mortal plane. And we are called to rise with our King and stand against the tide, not with weapons of this world but in the power of the Holy Spirit and with unbridled love for the lost. Will you stand?

Day 13

For God is Spirit, so those who worship him must worship in spirit and in truth.

John 4:24 (NLT)

How often do we try to confine God to our limited understanding? How often do we tell God that he can't do this or that? Yet, we seem to give Satan unlimited power. Are not both spirits? Yet, Isn't God the Creator? Isn't he the one that spoke all the universe, you and me, and Satan into existence? Why, then, do we try and confine God and limit him? Is it because we lack faith? Is it because we lean on fear rather than on trust? God is Spirit, and he is God: the Creator, the Master, the Architect, the All-Powerful. That is who we worship, not some minor spirit being or some physical human. So worship him today, as he truly is, and live in the victory that he has won.

Sitting down, Jesus called the Twelve and said, "Anyone who wants to be first must be the very last, and the servant of all."

Mark 9:35 (NIV)

No matter if it's in politics, work, ministry, family, school, or with God. If we deal with relationships, we are to be the first to be last. We have rights; due to our sins, we have the right to be condemned to eternal separation from God in hell. God has the right to carry out his justice and send his wrath upon our lives. We don't have the right to be first, to be the headliner. As followers of Jesus, our rights are left at the door to his will. To enter into salvation is to enter into an understanding that our rights are left behind so that God can take his rightful place as the author and finisher of our faith.

Jesus says to be last and put others first. His teaching flies in the face of everything society and within us has taught us. But it puts us in the right place for God's power to work in our lives.

So the question becomes, do you want to have your rights? Or do you want to be used by God?

Day 15

Be completely humble and gentle; be patient, bearing with one another in love.

Ephesians 4:2 (NIV)

What is your highest calling as a member of the Church? I'm not talking about a position you hold because you have attended a local body of believers for any particular amount of time. Or because you have completed an application and attended a new member's class. I'm talking about you as a member of Christ's body, the Church. As an adoptive son or daughter into the great family of God, you separate from a denomination, nation, and time period.

What is your highest calling as a member of that Church? Did you say to disciple? What if there's an even greater calling? What if I told you that we are called to make disciples of all the world but that there is a high calling as you, a member of the Church, have? Jesus prayed in Luke 17 not that our buildings would be significant, our music would be exciting, our preaching would be grand, or that our disciples would be many. Instead, Jesus prayed that our love would be evidence that God is real.

What is your highest calling as a member of the Church? That you would be unified with your brothers and sisters in Christ through the bond of love. But that means that our hobby horse theologies, our approaches to ministry, and our uniqueness in the body should never cause a divide among our brothers and sisters.

Instead, we are to bear with each other, to be patient, gentle, and humble. Our need to be correct must be left at the cross, and our more excellent need to show love must overcome our self-focused mentalities.

Are you fulfilling your highest calling, or is your membership to a building, a particular set of doctrines, a need to be right, keeping you from showing that God is real to lost people?

Day 16

You, Lord, are forgiving and good, abounding

in love to all who call to you.

Psalm 86:5 (NIV)

God is richly supplied in love—that's what abounding means. His forgiveness is rooted in this rich supply of love. From this never-ending well of love, God wipes away all our wrongs. And no wrong is too far from his love to forgive.

So don't let the voices of this world tell you that you're unforgivable, that there is a last straw that has broken God's love, that the well and supply of God's love has run out. It will never run out, and his forgiveness is fresh today for you.

Hear, O Israel: The Lord our God, the Lord is one. Love the Lord your God with all your heart and with all your soul and with all your strength.

Deuteronomy 6:4-5 (NIV)

Why would God tell us to love him with all our heart, soul, and strength, to which Jesus adds our mind in Mark 12:30? Is it not because we try to compartmentalize our love for him? Giving him aspects of ourselves rather than all of ourselves? Do we not have the tendency to try to merely feel him with our heart, or try to only think about him with our mind, or try to only serve him with our strengths, or try only to please him with our gifts?

We separate who we are and what we love him with so that we can control the other aspects we do not wish to give him. Yet, God calls us to love him with our whole being. With every aspect of who we are. Our heart with its emotions, our mind with its thoughts, our strength with all its energy, and our soul with all that God has created in us. When all our being is loving God in concert, then he is truly worshiped. In this, we show that we love him because everything of us is his.

That is what the Scriptures mean when they say, "No eye has seen, no ear has heard, and no mind has imagined what God has prepared for those who love him."

                                        1 Corinthians 2:9 (NLT)

The older we get, the harder it is for us to use our imagination. A child jumping from couch to couch not only sees lava, but they can feel the heat on their face.

We tend to become so weighed down by "reality" that our ability to imagine is hampered by our need to be "adults."

But it is in our imagination that we soar into God's possibilities. This is not to say that God resides in our imagination, but rather that it's in our imagination that we begin to shed our finite limitations and begin to understand God's limitless power, just as a child knows no bounds when seeing this world.

But I will sing of your strength, in the morning I will sing of your love; for you are my fortress, my refuge in times of trouble.

Psalm 59:16 (NIV)

Why sing of God in the morning? When an athlete competes, does he prepare on the field? When a soldier faces war, does he prepare when he sees the enemy? No, an athlete prepares months, even years, ahead of time for anything that could happen on the field. A soldier trains both physically and mentally before the enemy attacks.

Sing of God in the morning is the preparation we need to face the trials and battles that we will face all the day long. By training our eyes to focus on the God of our strength, we can face the battlefield of our lives, prepared for what it has in store for us. The question, then, is, have you stretched your vocal chords this morning? Go on and sing.

I love you, Lord, my strength. The Lord is my rock, my fortress and my deliverer; my God is my rock, in whom I take refuge, my shield and the horn of my salvation, my stronghold.

Psalm 18:1-2 (NIV)

In times of disorientation, how do you get oriented? In times of upheaval, how do you level off? In times of being overwhelmed, how do you find calm? God is the orienter, who gives us direction. God is the leveler, who puts us on straight roads. God is the calmer, who brings peace to our souls. In all things, God is ready to extend his strength, power, and shelter to anyone who understands their need for it.

Do you find yourself in a place where you feel weak, disoriented, thrown around, and exposed? Cry out to the God who wants to bring you onto straight roads to a place of

shelter in his presence.

For the word of the Lord is right and true; he is faithful in all he does. The Lord loves righteousness and justice; the earth is full of his unfailing love.

Psalm 33:4-5 (NIV)

I look around, and I have to say, I don't always see God's unfailing love. I don't always see what's right and true. I don't see righteousness and justice. Instead, I see unforgiveness running rampant in lives all around me. I see lies hold people's attention, hearts, and minds. I see corruption and lawlessness running from down the street to the halls of government and the courts.

And with all this, I can see why people ask, "Is God real?"

And then I remember Jesus' prayer for his disciples; in that prayer, the Church, those who have accepted Jesus' free gift of salvation, are to be people of love. They are to be people who are right and true. They are to live out righteousness and show justice. Why? Because they are his people and should reflect who God is. When we show love as God shows it, the unfailing kind, then people will know that he is real, and the Church will be the world changer it was created to be.

So, let's not look around and be consumed by the failings of this dying world but instead look to God so that we may become people who live in love, truth, righteousness, faithfulness, and justice.

Day 22

Do not those who plot evil go astray? But those who plan what is good find love and faithfulness.

Proverbs 14:22 (NIV)

Are you having a hard time? Does it feel like everything you do leads to heartbreak? Does it feel like your life is losing its meaning? Do you feel like things continue to crumble around you?

Some of the pain we experience in life is from outside sources. Yet, we bring many painful experiences upon ourselves. Why? We have a tendency to seek evil things—not because we're necessarily out to do evil, but rather because we are out for ourselves.

When seeking our benefit, we take our eyes off God and place them on ourselves.

When this happens, our intentions become mute, whether for the good or the bad; when our eyes are on ourselves, evil gains ground in our lives.

But if we keep our eyes on God and desire to do what he has told us to do in his Word, then we will not only be pursuing good but also find that we are fulfilled and that God's blessings flow out to us.

So, where are your eyes today?

We ought always to thank God for you, brothers and sisters, and rightly so, because your faith is growing more and more, and the love all of you have for one another is increasing.

2 Thessalonians 1:3 (NIV)

As the Church, our love for each other should grow and not wither. It should root itself firmly, not scatter in the wind. If we allow bitterness, pride, scheduling, personal quirks, or debatable theology to cut the rope of love that binds us together, then are we truly living the life that God has saved us to? If love isn't our primary goal, are we fulfilling Jesus' desire?

Instead of allowing ourselves to get in the way of the love we are called to, let us encourage each other, champion each other, and rejoice in each other. And let us thank God that he has brought us together as his Church, his

Body, his people. Let us be thankful that we are not our own, but we are his, and let us love each other with that in mind.

Day 24

If I speak in the tongues of men or of angels, but do not have love, I am only a resounding gong or a clanging cymbal. If I have the gift of prophecy and can fathom all mysteries and all knowledge, and if I have a faith that can move mountains, but do not have love, I am nothing. If I give all I possess to the poor and give over my body to hardship that I may boast, but do not have love, I gain nothing.

1 Corinthians 13:1-3 (NIV)

Have you ever thought about what you'll take into eternity with you? It's not like you're going on a camping trip, where you'll need clothes, swimwear, sunscreen, tents, food, etc. In eternity, we'll take nothing of this world with us. We won't even take most of our theology with us. Think about it: in eternity, will the doctrine of the rapture matter? What about predestination? Tongues? Prophecy? What about our approaches to music? Preaching style? Evangelism? Classes? Church organization?

What will we take? Knowledge of the True God. Jesus, our Savior, came to earth through the prophesied virgin, lived a perfect life, died, and is at the right hand of the Father. Our salvation is by trusting in Jesus alone for our acceptance into the family of God. The Church, our brothers and sisters from every nation and tongue, have confessed Jesus as Lord. Love, the bond that Jesus calls us into, shows that we are his and that he is real.

Let's put this world into perspective, leaving behind the things that will not matter in eternity and clinging to those things that will.

Today, what are you clinging to? Is it more of a need to be right or humble yourself to the God of the Universe?

Love is patient, love is kind. It does not envy, it does not boast, it is not proud. It does not dishonor others, it is not self-seeking, it is not easily angered, it keeps no record of wrongs.

1 Corinthians 13:4-5 (NIV)

Look around, in our politics, in our jobs, in our families, in our churches; what do you see? Do we see people who are quick to anger? Do we see jealousy? Do we see people puff themselves up? Do we see pride? Do we see disrespect? Do we see people out for their own good?

Love does the opposite of what we see, which is why the love of God is so radical. It flies in the face of what we see every day in all facets of society and culture. When the people of God truly live the love that God has called us to, the world is dramatically changed.

But God's people have a tendency to look at the world and record all the problems that we see. And we fall lock-step with how the world works and are opposed to the way God works.

Today, are you ready to take the radical step of loving like God loves? It means putting away yourself and letting God work.

Day 26

Love does not delight in evil but rejoices with the truth. It always protects, always trusts, always hopes, always perseveres.

1 Corinthians 13:6-7 (NIV)

Protection, have you ever thought that protection doesn't necessarily mean concealment? Concealment can be good; Oskar Schindler, during the Nazi era, concealed Jews from death through his factory. Jacob Howard helped escaping black men and women in the Underground Railroad so they could escape their slavery. Concealment, for a godly cause, can be to protect people from harm.

Yet, far too often, we think that if we conceal bad behavior, we are protecting someone. But in reality, all we're doing is aiding them in their things that will lead to destruction. Should I keep it to myself if I know a person whose spouse is physically abusing them? Should I keep it to myself if I know of a child who is being sexually abused? Should I keep it to myself if I know a friend who is a drug addict? Should I keep it to myself if I know someone who is on the verge of suicide?

Is concealing those things helpful? Of course not! Usually, concealment masquerades itself as a false sense of protection when, in reality, all it does is cause more destruction in the lives of everyone involved.

Love does not conceal lies. Love does not conceal evil. Love uncovers those things that are being hidden so that the lies around us can be dealt with. And true protection can accrue.

Are you showing love with your concealment, or are you showing destruction?

Day 27

This is love: not that we loved God, but that he loved us and sent his Son as an atoning sacrifice for our sins.

1 John 4:10 (NIV)

Have you ever wondered if you really knew what love is? We might think we understand love, but our society equates it to emotion, a physical act, gift-giving, and words. In reality, even our deepest experience of love is only a shadow of what true love is.

True love is sacrificial, but it does not mean just giving up something for someone. Instead, it means giving up everything for them, seeking their good above and beyond your own, and caring more for their well-being than for your own.

This is what love is: God the Son descends from perfection into imperfection. This is what love is then: God the Son descends from eternal praise of who he is and places himself in a position to be rejected by his creation. This is what love is: God the Son descends from eternity into finite existence. This is what love is then: God the Son descends from life immeasurable into death undeserving.

Until we can begin to love in this way, how can we begin to think that we understand what love is?

For this is the message you heard from the beginning: We should love one another.

1 John 3:11 (NIV)

What do you think the point of your faith is? Is it that you get to go to heaven? Is it that you are going to become a better person? Is it that you get to have peace that passes all understanding?

What if, instead, the point of your faith was that you were to be the recipient of God's love and the conduit of that love to others?

What would change in your Christian walk if nothing mattered more than the love of God for both yourself and for the people around you?

Can anything ever separate us from Christ's love? Does it mean he no longer loves us if we have trouble or calamity, or are persecuted, or hungry, or destitute, or in danger, or threatened with death? No, despite all these things, overwhelming victory is ours through Christ, who loved us.

Romans 8:35 (NLT)

What if, just what if, we loved the people around us like Christ loves us? What if, no matter what the situation, no matter what their theological stance, no matter what their actions communicate, we still loved them?

What would happen, not only in our relationships with those people but also in our relationships with God?

Let's move away from what-ifs and start living it. What do you think?

For I am convinced that neither death nor life, neither angels nor demons, neither the present nor the future, nor any powers, neither height nor depth, nor anything else in all creation, will be able to separate us from the love of God that is in Christ Jesus our Lord.

Romans 8:38-39 (NIV)

Do you feel like you're not good enough? That you don't live up to the standards of the Church? Do you feel like you fall short of the expectations of your Pastor? Do you feel that because of your shortcomings, God is turning his back on you when you mess up?

But do you realize that you are his if you have placed your trust in Jesus? Every sin you have committed, are committing and will commit has been paid for? That you are God's? No power in this or the spiritual world can destroy the reality that you have been brought into the family of God.

Instead of listening to the voice that says you don't make the cut, live in the reality surrounding you. Those Church standards you can't live up to are an illusion; the Church was built by Jesus, who had you in mind when he created it. It is a place where redeemed sinners gather to worship a holy God. Your belief that the Pastor is judging and waiting for you to fall short is an illusion. The vast majority of pastors want to see the Holy Spirit at work in your life and desire to help you realize it. Those times you have messed up are a stepping stone; they can either hinder you or point you to a deeper understanding of the love of God.

Nothing, no nothing, can take you away from God, except when you believe the lies that say something can. Today, trust in the God who died for you so that nothing can take you from his arms.

Day 31

There is no fear in love. But perfect love drives out fear, because fear has to do with punishment. The one who fears is not made perfect in love.

1 John 4:18 (NIV)

You and I were made to love in a way that has no concept of rejection. When God created us, there was no backbiting, no trying to figure out what someone else was trying to say, and no getting hurt by not doing all the right things; it was simply love. And in true godly love, there is no fear of rejection, no fear of getting it wrong, and no fear of punishment. It is simply love; love sacrifices oneself for another. Love puts another's needs above their own. Love that pushes through any difficult situation.

Love also says I will do what is necessary to show love, whether that means doing something new or something hard. In God's love, the love we were created to experience and give out, fear has no power, therefore we should not fear to love.

Jesus replied, "'You must love the Lord your God with all your heart, all your soul, and all your mind.' This is the first and greatest commandment. A second is equally important: 'Love your neighbor as yourself.'"

Matthew 22:37-39 (NLT)

Sometimes, I get to thinking about all the celebrities out there who are making it in the world. You know what I mean by making it, right? They have the money, influence, houses, cars, and glamor.

Yet the one thing I don't see many celebrities have is a noticeable relationship with Jesus. Sure, they might reference him, but there's no out-and-out proclaiming him through word and action.

Instead, most celebrities, even those that mention Jesus positively, live the exact opposite life that he calls humanity to. And yet they are thriving. They have the money, the fame, and the influence. And I think to myself, why?

Why does God allow people who are set against him to thrive? Why do people who live for themselves and their self-proclamation seem to thrive, yet those who follow God seem to suffer?

And then I remember that if Jesus suffered, we, his followers, will also suffer. I also remember that celebrities are not thriving. Drugs, depression, alcoholism, and the constant need to be on the cutting edge drive most celebrities to the breaking point. Rehabs are abundant, self-help is everywhere, and the stories of celebrities falling victim to the corrupt world they inhabit have created an industry that exploits their downfall.

Yet those who choose to follow Jesus and seek the good of others may not have the money or the status; what they have is a God who sees them and who works out the suffering they are going through for good.

Jesus' followers will likely thrive, not in finances, but in love and acceptance.

So, never look to the celebrities of this world and say, "I want that," because it will fail. Instead, look to Jesus and desire him because, in all things, he will not fail.

Day 33

"For I know the plans I have for you," declares the Lord, "plans to prosper you and not to harm you, plans to give you hope and a future. Then you will call on me and come and pray to me, and I will listen to you. You will seek me and find me when you seek me with all your heart."

Jeremiah 29:11-13 (NIV)

Here's a short thought in between to big ones. When we submit to God's plans for our lives, we find him. Then, we can call upon him, and he will listen to us. Until we are ready to live our lives for him, we cannot expect to know the God of the universe in a personal relationship.

For God did not send his Son into the world to condemn the world, but to save the world through him.

John 3:17 (NIV)

"God is out to get me." Ever feel that way? You ask God for something, and then it seems like a bunch of bad things happen. Or, you think life is going well, and then one day, you learn that a lot of what you thought was good was just people putting on masks to hide their true actions. "Why did God allow it?" we ask ourselves.

Sometimes, the hardest truth to struggle with is that God always wants the best in our lives. Sometimes, that means that the road to the best drives through valleys of hurt.

Because of the sinfulness of man, we are not simply navigating through spread-out icebergs. The reality is this world is a constant storm that swirls all around us. At times, we find the eye of the storm where there's peace, but because of sin, we don't stay there for long.

The actions of the people around us, coupled with our own, produce these storms. But it is God who desires to bring us into clear and calm waters. But in order to get to those waters, we must weather the storms.

Instead of asking God "why," shouldn't we cry out to God to take control? When we ask why, we're saying he doesn't know, but when we hand over the wheel of our ship to him, we're acknowledging that God knows the route through the storm. When the Captain guides the ship, peace will come with the calm waters ahead.

This is how God showed his love among us: He sent his one and only Son into the world that we might live through him.

>1 John 4:9 (NIV)

We say, God, give me a bigger bank account. God, give me a better job. God, give me a more loving family. God, give me a cooler car. GOD give me…God GIVE me…God give ME…

God replies: You were given love; I was given a cross. You were given forgiveness; I was given spit, thorns, and a whip. You were given new life; I was given undeserved pain and suffering. You are given the free gift of grace; I was given death at the hands of my creation. We both have gained you the opportunity to live with me eternally, and I have the opportunity for you to live with me eternally. What do we have in common? You, Me, and eternity.

My question: Do we take the opportunity, or do we continue to ask for meaningless things from the God who has given us so much already?

Day 36

"My thoughts are nothing like your thoughts," says the Lord. "And my ways are far beyond anything you could imagine. For just as the heavens are higher than the earth, so my ways are higher than your ways and my thoughts higher than your thoughts."

Isaiah 55:8-9 (NLT)

Do you know what a command is? Here's the dictionary definition of command: "the possession or exercise of controlling authority: to direct with specific authority or prerogative; order…"

For those who have been around any type of military or, at the very least, have been on a team where a command is given, it must be carried out. There is no option; the command must be done. Why is that? Why must people carry out the commands of their commander? I mean, what will it really hurt if a command goes undone?

If a commander in war tells his troops to be at a particular place at a specific time and they're not, what's the big deal? If a coach tells his team to set up a certain way, and they don't, what's it really going to affect?

If you're on a sports team, you can lose the game if you don't listen to your coach. That's because the coach can see the whole field and anticipate the other team's actions, and you, being a player, might not have the same view. The other team can get the upper hand if his commands are not followed. In war, if a commander's orders are not followed, the enemy can get the upper hand, and people could die.

Commands are essential to follow because the commander is looking out for their troops and the betterment of all those under his command.

When God commands us not to be afraid and to have courage, what's the big deal if we don't? There's nothing to be won; life and death are not hanging in the balance, so what's the big deal?

Though we might not be on the playing field of a game or the battlefield of a war, we live day in and day out in the fields of our lives where the outcome of our lives in eternity is being won or lost. When we take God's commands seriously, follow through on those commands, and implement them in our lives, we show our trust in God. By doing so, we stand for him and guide others to the saving work of Jesus.

When hard times come, when people belittle us, families struggle, and the commands of God are carried out, God is glorified, and our faith grows. In those times of peril, we can stand secure in God's life because we are marching in line with his commands.

So, "… Be strong and courageous. Do not be afraid; do not be discouraged, for the Lord your God will be with you wherever you go. (Josh 1:9, [NIV])"

Go and do it.

For the Lord himself will come down from heaven, with a loud command, with the voice of the archangel and with the trumpet call of God, and the dead in Christ will rise first. After that, we who are still alive and are left will be caught up together with them in the clouds to meet the Lord in the air. And so we will be with the Lord forever.

                                        1 Thessalonians 4:16-17 (NIV)

Where does your hope rest? In the temporary world around you? In the tasks that you accomplish day-to-day? Or does your hope rest on the return of Jesus?

Where our hope rests is reflected in where we put our hands to work. If we work just to make our lives better, we are working for the temporary. If we work just to leave good things to our children, our work is for this world. But, if we work to make others come to a saving knowledge of Jesus, our work is for the eternal. If we are working to be used by God to build his kingdom, then we are working for his return.

If we desire to make our hope rest on Jesus' return, our lives must reflect it. Let us look at all we do and ask one simple question, "Is this worthy to show Jesus when he returns, or not?"

Let us be people who have hope in Jesus' return and go about our lives working for it.

But in your hearts revere Christ as Lord. Always be prepared to give an answer to everyone who asks you to give the reason for the hope that you have. But do this with gentleness and respect …

1 Peter 3:15 (NIV)

How well do you know your faith? I mean, the faith that has been passed down from Christian to Christian since the Apostles? Do you know what has caused division? What has unified? Do you know at least the basic teachings of your faith? Can you put into words why you believe that Jesus has saved you? Could you explain how and why you came to know who Jesus is?

All Christians, not just pastors or missionaries, are called by God to know who he is and be able to tell others about our experience with him. We must be able to clearly relate that he's real, how we came to know Jesus as our

Savior, why we trust him, and that he's coming again.

It is also a good skill for all Christians to have an overview of the history of Christianity and its teachings so that they can have informed conversations with others.

The question is, how much effort have you put into your faith? You don't have to be a scholar, but you are called to be a relayer. Someone who can have a meaningful conversation about their faith with someone seeking to understand why you have hope in Jesus.

So, ask yourself, "Would I be able to have a meaningful conversation about Jesus?" If so, I encourage you to learn as much as you can. If not, I would encourage you to pick up a book about the history of Christianity or fundamental beliefs and begin to discover the why of your hope and the history behind it.

Know therefore that the Lord your God is God;

he is the faithful God, keeping his covenant of

love to a thousand generations of those who

love him and keep his commandments.

Deuteronomy 7:9 (NIV)

Do you know God? Do you know that he is real? Do you know that he loves you? Do you know that he created you for a purpose? Did you know that he is active in this world? In your life? Do you know that he will always be by your side? Did you know that you can love him? Please him?

You were created by a God who wants to lavish his love and blessings on you. He is real and active, and he will never leave you. He created you for a purpose that you can only discover by accepting him as your Savior and living out his commands. You were created to do those two things.

But you need to know him, experience him, and solidify yourself in the reality that God is God, and you are his. Have you?

For this very reason, make every effort to add to your faith goodness; and to goodness, knowledge; and to knowledge, self-control; and to self-control, perseverance; and to perseverance, godliness; and to godliness, mutual affection; and to mutual affection, love. For if you possess these qualities in increasing measure, they will keep you from being ineffective and unproductive in your knowledge of our Lord Jesus Christ.

2 Peter 1:5-8 (NIV)

Do you like math? Some of us are very good at it. There are those people who can almost physically see the problem unfolding in front of them. Then there are other people who cringe at the very mention of math and get by just with basic addition and subtraction.

In our relationship with God, there is a type of math that none of us should shrink away from. Addition of the good qualities that we were saved to produce, and subtraction of sin. Our faith is the basis on which all the goodness of God is added. From our faith in the God who saves us by his grace, we are to add the goodness of him. The knowledge of his will, the self-control of our actions, the perseverance in difficult circumstances, the godliness of a transformed life, the unity of affection towards each other as we understand that we're all in this together, and the love that has been poured out on us and in turn we show to others.

We are to add these things to our lives through the power of the Holy Spirit, who indwells us. And as these are added into our lives, we become better equipped to be used by God to reach this world. The question then becomes, have you seen these things being added to your life? Are you trying just to get by in them?

then know this, you and all the people of Israel: It is by the name of Jesus Christ of Nazareth, whom you crucified but whom God raised from the dead, that this man stands before you healed … Salvation is found in no one else, for there is no other name under heaven given to mankind by which we must be saved.

Acts 4:10,12 (NIV)

Do you own the crucifixion? There are two ways of owning it. The first leads to the second. Most of us cling to the second, with a semi-acknowledgment of the first.

This second ownership of the crucifixion is to thank God that because of Christ's crucifixion, we have been brought from death to life. We can be in a right relationship with God by his grace, not based on what we have done. Each of us is to own the crucifixion like this because God is to be praised for saving sinners like us.

But go deeper than that, own it more than before. You and I are the cause of the crucifixion. By our deeds, we drove the nails into Christ's flesh. By our deeds, we pierced the side of Christ. By our deeds, we mocked and ridiculed him as he hung. And by our deeds, we laid upon him a crown of thorns. In Scripture, Peter says, "Whom you crucified." I crucified Christ. I hung him on the cross. "It was my sin that kept him there," as the hymn says. I own that, and it brings greater appreciation for his sacrifice. Because he did no wrong, but my wrong killed him.

Do you own the crucifixion like this? Christ, "whom you crucified," did it out of his desire to bring you back to him, and for that, he is to be praised. Amen.

Therefore, as God's chosen people, holy and dearly loved, clothe yourselves with compassion, kindness, humility, gentleness and patience.

Colossians 3:12 (NIV)

What are you wearing right now? Jeans, shorts, T-shirt, shoes with socks, flip-flops? Okay, how much did all that cost? How much of your hard-earned or someone else's hard-earned money did it cost? Did you have to settle for a pair of jeans that wasn't the best because you didn't have enough money? What about your shoes? Did you finally get the shoes you always wanted, but now you don't have any more money to spend?

There's a cost for every piece of clothing that we wear. The cost of the clothes God wants us to wear is the cost of Jesus on the cross. The cost of compassion is nails through Jesus' hands. The cost of kindness is nails through his feet. The cost of humility is a crown of thorns on a head. The cost of gentleness is a whip against flesh. The cost of patience is the hours spent bleeding on a splintered cross.

God desires us to clothe ourselves with the finest things, which he could buy through Jesus's death on the cross. So, have you put on the clothes that God has bought for you?

Day 43

The Lord is my shepherd; I shall not want. He makes me lie down in green pastures. He leads me beside still waters. He restores my soul. He leads me in paths of righteousness for his name's sake.

Psalm 23:1-3 (ESV)

If God is our Shepherd and we are the sheep that should follow him, what's the point?

What's the point of following God? Sometimes, we tend to view following God from a "how does it benefit me" way. I mean, Psalm 23 gives us many benefits that come with following God. Let's look at some of them:

"Shall not want," Shepherds had to supply the sheep with food, water, and protection. God supplies our needs so we don't have to worry.

"Lie down in green pastures." Shepherds try to find the best places for their sheep to relax because sheep are so skittish. So, there's comfort in God. He stills our souls in the storms of life and brings us peace.

"He leads me beside still waters," Shepherds would temper streams and make pools for their sheep to drink from, which means that even in the chaos that can happen in our lives, God can calm it.

"He restores my soul. "When we feel empty, dry, and close to death, God brings life to us to keep us going.

"He leads me in paths of righteousness," In God's eyes, there's a right way to live this life and a wrong way. God's way is the right way, and if we follow the paths he lays out for us, we will stand tall, though we may have troubles.

We can get these benefits from following God, but we can't miss the point. The point is not what we can get from God but what it's all for. At the end of verse 3 of Psalm 23, it says, "for his name's sake." What is the point of God providing all this for us? Is it just so we can get through this life? No, it's so that he can be known to the world.

Our benefits are not for us but for the people around us to know that there is a God in heaven and that he is active in our lives today. We can take God's benefits and use them in two ways: We can use them for God's glory or abuse them for our own. The question is, which one will we choose?

May the God of hope fill you with all joy and peace as you trust in him, so that you may overflow with hope by the power of the Holy Spirit.

                                        Romans 15:13 (NIV)

Where does your hope in the Father's love come from? Where does your hope in Jesus' saving ability come from? Doesn't it come from the Holy Spirit? Doesn't it come from him working in your life? Doesn't it come from him revealing the Father's love for you? Doesn't it come from experiencing the freedom that Jesus gave you?

The Holy Spirit wants you to know and experience the God of hope and be filled with that hope. Only when we allow the Holy Spirit to do his job and transform us can we begin to have a solid relationship with God as a whole.

Let us not shy away from his movement but rather seek it.

Day 45

But the Holy Spirit produces this kind of fruit in our lives: love, joy, peace, patience, kindness, goodness, faithfulness, gentleness, and self-control. There is no law against these things!

Galatians 5:22-23 (NLT)

Here's the hard truth: if you've been a "Christian" for a number of years, if you have gone to church, sat on a board, heard the sermons, and sang the songs, but you haven't seen the fruits of the Holy Spirit manifest in your life, then you're living out a religion, not a relationship with Jesus.

Turn away from religion, turn towards Jesus, reject the act of religious works, and embrace the work of the Holy Spirit.

Day 46

But blessed is the one who trusts in the Lord, whose confidence is in him. They will be like a tree planted by the water that sends out its roots by the stream. It does not fear when heat comes; its leaves are always green. It has no worries in a year of drought and never fails to bear fruit.

Jeremiah 17:7-8 (NIV)

This world can throw a lot at us: loss of job, trouble in school, marital strife, family squabbles, abuse, drug use, natural disasters, death, and the list can go on and on. No one is immune to trouble. It doesn't matter if you do not have one cent to your name or are the richest person with fans everywhere; we all experience the trouble this world has to offer.

Yet, God calls us not to a life without trouble but a life where trouble increases. Why? One would think that the God who says he wants to give us peace would provide us with a life of ease. Being all-powerful, one would think that God would provide us with a life fully protected against all the bad that would come against us. But that is not what he does. Instead, his desire is for us to rely on him. That when trouble comes, we turn to him and trust him. We express our worries and fears to him and then trust that he is working.

Why does he intend this rather than exempting us from trouble? It is twofold: First, it is to build our relationship with him. How can we trust him if we are never given the opportunity to do so? Second, it is to show others who do not know God that, though they have trouble, God can rest them from the worry it brings.

If we turn to God in trouble, rather than to worry or self-reliance, we experience a gift of God that goes beyond any assurance or peace this world has to offer. Just like a tree, whose roots are connected to water, no trouble will trouble us because our source of sustenance is always intact.

A final word: Be strong in the Lord and in his mighty power. Put on all of God's armor so that you will be able to stand firm against all strategies of the devil.

Ephesians 6:10-11 (NLT)

Be strong, not in your knowledge or physical or mental strength. "Be strong in the Lord and in his mighty power."

Everything that we turn to in this world, whether it be self-help books, secular psychological therapies, occult practices like astrology, or sex, drugs, and alcohol. They all have one thing in common: they're a strength or a source of reprieve outside the realm of God.

Why do we do it? Because it's easier to have something submit to us where we think we hold the power. It seems we like the illusion of being in control, having ourselves as the ones who can manipulate the things around us. But the reality is that we are the puppets; we are the ones attached by strings. It is an illusion to think that we are the puppeteers that we make these things dance for us.

Rather, God tells us to be strong, not in our delusion, but in the reality that only when we willingly submit to him do we find true strength, freedom, and a release from the strings that control us. And here is the paradox: only through submission to God can freedom be attained.

Day 48

God blesses those who patiently endure testing and temptation. Afterward they will receive the crown of life that God has promised to those who love him.

James 1:12 (NLT)

Tests of any kind can be excruciating. Whether we're studying for a school examination, preparing for a performance review, or preparing for a job interview, we tend to shy away, worry, or feel nervous because tests, by their nature, push us out of our comfort zone by challenging us in unknown ways.

Yet, it's the tests that drive us to achieve. It's the test that grows us as a person. It's the test that doesn't allow us to stay complacent but moves us closer to victory. Even a failure on a test teaches us how to overcome it in the future.

God understands the need for testing in our lives because we retreat to ourselves and away from him without it. That's why he blesses us when we embrace the test, understanding that it is good for our lives.

Here are two hints for every test you will face: When in doubt, choose "C," and the answer to every test not on paper is simply to trust God.

For the wages of sin is death, but the gift of

God is eternal life in Christ Jesus our Lord.

Romans 6:23 (NIV)

"Two roads diverged in a yellow wood…" the famous opening lines from Robert Frost's poem, "The Road Not Taken." In the poem, Frost believes either is acceptable, and he is sad that he can only take one.

There are also two roads that diverge in our heart. One is the road of self. It is marked with suffering and leads to death. It is the most traversed one. The one that is wider and, at first glance, looks the best, but in the end, it's the path that leads to destruction and separation from God forever.

The second road is the submission of a will. It's a road also marked with suffering, but this one leads to life. This one is less traversed. It is narrower and seems at first the harder of the two to begin on. But as one ventures down it, joy and peace will be found because, with this road, the Savior also walks and guides us to eternity with God.

The question is, which road will you traverse?

Day 50

If we confess our sins, he is faithful and just and will forgive us our sins and purify us from all unrighteousness.

1 John 1:9 (NIV)

All. You know, that word gets used all the time. See, it just happened. We use a lot of the time to point out someone's flaws. We say things like, "They talk bad about me all the time." or we use its friend, always. "You always leave the seat up." But the reality is that all and always, are not always true. Because if even once, that person didn't say anything bad about us or didn't leave the toilet seat up, then our all and always is false.

But with God, all and always is always correct. So when the Bible says that God will purify us, cleaning us from all our sins, guess what? He does it all the time. So if we confess, then he will always cleanse.

That's a good use of the word all, don't you think?

For you have been given not only the privilege of trusting in Christ but also the privilege of suffering for him.

Philippians 1:29 (NLT)

Suffering, a privilege? Yep, because if you're suffering for following Jesus, it means you're his, and will live forever in eternity.

Now, if you're suffering because you're a jerk, yeah, you deserve it. And it means you need a course correction back to God.

Either way, follow Jesus.

On God rests my salvation and my glory; my

mighty rock, my refuge is God.

Psalm 62:7 (ESV)

Growing up in the world of sports, you see many, and I mean a lot, of injuries. Ranging from a slight cramp to broken bones. It's not uncommon to walk down a high school corridor during any sports season and see an athlete resting on crutches. Many people know the feeling of resting on those crutches, trusting they will hold your strength. I've seen people try to use crutches to get up, and they end up falling because the crutches were not steady enough and just gave out from underneath them.

But why do we need crutches when we get hurt? Because we're injured and cannot support ourselves, we use crutches to steady ourselves and help in the healing process.

I've heard it said that people use Jesus as a crutch because they are too weak to make it on their own. I agree. I am too weak, I am injured, I am broken, I need support, I need to be steadied, I need healing.

Working with people for the last few decades, I realize we're all broken, hurting, and weak. We all need support and crutches to lean on. I look around, and I see people leaning on many things: alcohol, drugs, relationships, approval, careers. We are all in need, and we are all hurting.

We seek people's approval to let us know that we're good enough, and when the people around us don't give it to us, we feel empty and abandoned. We need something to delight us.

Every day, we are taught new ideas that change and contradict the ideas we were taught yesterday. So we get confused and turned around. We need solid teachings and guidance. We limp around this world, trying to weather the storms and get beaten from all sides. We all need a refuge.

I am crippled in my life, I am hurt, I am in need, and I don't care if others don't get it because Jesus gets it. In him, I find rest; in him,

I find acceptance; in him, I find solid ground; and in him, I find my refuge from storms. He is my crutch because I need healing.

Take a look at yourself and be truthful. Do you have it all together? Are you looking for approval, healing, or an anchor in this world? Can you say you're strong enough to get through all this world offers?

If we're honest with ourselves, we can all agree that we're hurt, in pain, and need support. Jesus is the healing, the support we need, but we need to lean on him and his words just like the athlete leans on his crutch for healing.

For there is one God and one mediator between God and mankind, the man Christ Jesus, who gave himself as a ransom for all people. This has now been witnessed to at the proper time.

1 Timothy 2:5-6 (NIV)

No one should stand between you and God. Not a pastor, priest, small group leader, mentor, etc. You and I can go straight to God without any clergy or stand-in for him.

We are here to help each other wrestle with God's word, encourage each other to become more deeply connected to him, and stand with each other when this life gets hard. But none of us is a substitute for the Living God. None of us can say that we have more access to his throne. All have the opportunity to come before the God of Creation to learn, seek, and find.

Is someone trying to step between you and God? Is there something telling you that you can't go directly to him? You can go directly to God's throne, and you can experience all that he has saved you, too.

God made him who had no sin to be sin for us,

so that in him we might become the

righteousness of God.

2 Corinthians 5:21 (NIV)

Jesus ≠ sin. Jesus ↦ sin ▪ us. That we might ≡ God's righteousness.

But have you been ♻ by Jesus?

Day 55

He was despised and rejected by mankind, a man of suffering, and familiar with pain. Like one from whom people hide their faces he was despised, and we held him in low esteem. Surely he took up our pain and bore our suffering, yet we considered him punished by God, stricken by him, and afflicted.

Isaiah 53:3-4 (NIV)

The prophet Isaiah wrote about the Messiah roughly 900 years before Jesus fulfilled his prophecies. Isaiah said that Jesus would be held in low esteem. We see this time and time again. Though Jesus radically changed the course of human history, countless people hold him in low esteem.

When some says they believe Jesus was a good teacher, yet reject that he taught that he was God, they show they hold him in low esteem.

Every time a person calls on the name of Jesus for help and then turns around and uses his name as a cuss word, they show they still hold him in low esteem.

And every time we confess to being a Christian yet think sin has greater power than him, we hold him in low esteem.

Jesus is the God of the Universe. He has the Name above all names. He is the infinite Alpha and Omega. Let us treat him in high esteem by submitting to who he is rather than trying to make him submit to us.

But he was pierced for our transgressions, he was crushed for our iniquities; the punishment that brought us peace was on him, and by his wounds we are healed. We all, like sheep, have gone astray, each of us has turned to our own way; and the Lord has laid on him the iniquity of us all.

Isaiah 53:5-6 (NIV)

Pierced, crushed, punished, peace, healed. Five words that do not seem to go with each other. Yet, five words that are needed. These five words show the love of God. These five words show our need. These five words show our past, our present, and our future. These five words bring us back, restore us, and show that there is victory for us. Why? Because three of these words speak of one man, God in the flesh, providing the way for two words to become truth in us.

The fool says in his heart, "There is no God."

They are corrupt, their deeds are vile; there is no one who does good.

> Psalm 14:1 (NIV)

On April Fool's Day, let's call good evil and evil good. Let us call corruption justice and justice corruption. Let us call the things that destroy lives worth it and those that will strengthen lives a hindrance.

But here's the thing: April Fool's Day wouldn't be just one day a year. Instead, as our world moves down the wide path, we see that we live in a world where evil is the new good, and good is now decried as evil. April Fool's Day has moved from one day in a calendar year to a social norm of rebellion against God.

"God is dead, and we have killed him." Friedrich Nietzsche. The fools have spoken, stand up today denying the foolishness of this world, and embrace the wisdom that only comes from the Creator.

For Christ's love compels us, because we are convinced that one died for all, and therefore all died. And he died for all, that those who live should no longer live for themselves but for him who died for them and was raised again.

2 Corinthians 5:14-15 (NIV)

To compel, effect, motivate, precipitate, launch. Christ's love takes us from one place of being to another. From one path of this world to another. We are jettisoned away from living for ourselves and set on the path of living for him. Instead of trying to return to the place where we have been moved from, instead of returning to our old existence, let us live the new life. Let us live for the One that brought us from death into life. Let us live in the risen life of servanthood to Christ rather than in the coffin of self-infatuation.

This is how we know what love is: Jesus Christ laid down his life for us. And we ought to lay down our lives for our brothers and sisters.

1 John 3:16 (NIV)

"This is how we know what love is: Jesus Christ laid down his life for us." Not by the miracles that God does. Not by the communication that God has with us. Not by the leather-bound Bibles we carry. Not by the buildings we erect, the music we play, or the sermons that are preached. All those can add to our understanding of the love of God, but if God did nothing other than send Jesus to die for us, then we have all we need to know about what love is.

Day 60

I have been crucified with Christ and I no longer live, but Christ lives in me. The life I now live in the body, I live by faith in the Son of God, who loved me and gave himself for me.

Galatians 2:20 (NIV)

It's time to walk as the living dead. We are dead, crucified, and buried with Christ. Sin has no power over us, people's opinions about us have no power over us, this world has no authority over us; we are dead to it all. But we are raised to new life in Christ. The life of joy, peace, patience, kindness, gentleness, self-control, humility, love, self-sacrifice, eternal living.

But do you trust, having faith that it is true? That's the question because the reality is, if you have accepted and put your trust in Jesus as your Savior, you are the living-dead, dead to sin, but alive in Christ.

For if, while we were God's enemies, we were reconciled to him through the death of his Son, how much more, having been reconciled, shall we be saved through his life!

Romans 5:10 (NIV)

Imagine that one person who has been upsetting you lately and would be considered an enemy. Maybe they've done something that hurt you, got you in trouble, or said something that you didn't like. On a scale of 1 through 10, 10 being with forgiveness and 1 being murder, how did you handle it? With us, God treated us like a 10, but then one step further and showed us an 11.

See, he handled us with mercy and grace. God showed mercy to us by putting his wrath on Jesus when Jesus died on the cross. This mercy part was the 10, and like him, we are to show the same forgiveness and mercy to others as has been shown to us. But it doesn't stop there. God shows grace by extending us not just mercy in the grave but grace to eternal life. God treats us as an 11. Mercy shows restraint, and grace goes beyond restraint by giving a gift that is not deserved.

We tend to treat people with 7s or lower, but God calls us to be 11s. Showing not just mercy and forgiveness, but going beyond that into the realm of looking to benefit them, even in their acts of meanness toward us.

It's hard, and we'll experience hurt and suffering because of it, but God does it for us. How can we think we're better than him?

Day 62

"He himself bore our sins" in his body on the cross, so that we might die to sins and live for righteousness; "by his wounds you have been healed."

1 Peter 2:24 (NIV)

Jesus did not take our sins onto himself so that we would no longer have them. He took on our sins so that we may live—not live life in excess, nor live life without care, but rather, live life in its fullness.

That fullness of life is life that begins at the starting point of the cross, with God as the guide through our life's journey and God as the end goal. Jesus took on our sins so that we may live the way God has designed us to live, as God originally created us to live. And that life is lived through obedience to God's right way of living, which is trusting in him and following what he says is good.

Our sins were taken on for this purpose so we may know and experience the full life we were created to live. Are you living God's full life?

Day 63

Then he said to the crowd, "If any of you wants to be my follower, you must give up your own way, take up your cross daily, and follow me. If you try to hang on to your life, you will lose it. But if you give up your life for my sake, you will save it."

Luke 9:23-24 (NLT)

Do you have desires? Dreams? A plan? Guess what? If it doesn't align with God's, it's not going to work. God has a direction he's going; we can either get on board with it or jump back in the water. There is no halfway with God. We can't give him only what we think we should and expect him to be fine with that. No, he wants it all. All of our heart, all of our mind, all of our strength, and all of our soul.

If we're not ready to lay down our arms against him and surrender every aspect of ourselves to the One that created and bought us, how can we expect to follow him rightly?

For everyone has sinned; we all fall short of God's glorious standard. Yet God, in his grace, freely makes us right in his sight. He did this through Christ Jesus when he freed us from the penalty for our sins.

>Romans 3:23-24 (NLT)

What is your standard of morality for the people around you? Don't smoke? Don't drink? Don't have premarital or extramarital sex? Don't lie, steal, gossip, or maybe play cards. What happens when someone doesn't line up with our standard of morality? Do we curse them, reject them, or disassociate ourselves from them?

What about God's standard? Ever hate someone in your heart? Ever want something that isn't yours? Ever spend more time with an object as your goal to the detriment of everything else?

What does God do for us when we don't meet his standard? He frees us from the eternal penalty of our failure. He shows us grace and makes us be able to stand before him. He calls us his sons and daughters.

No matter who we are, no matter our age, gender, or economic and societal status, we are loved by God. And he has done everything needed to bring us back into a right relationship. How can we deny that to those who don't fit our standards? We can't.

Day 65

Now, brothers and sisters, I want to remind you of the gospel I preached to you, which you received and on which you have taken your stand. For what I received I passed on to you as of first importance: that Christ died for our sins according to the Scriptures, that he was buried, that he was raised on the third day according to the Scriptures,

                    1 Corinthians 15:1, 3-4 (NIV)

According to the Scriptures, Christ had to die. Jesus died because it was God's plan for him to die. Jesus died because he desired to carry out that plan. Jesus died because God loves us, even in our rebellion against him. This was not some plan that started in a stable in Bethlehem or on the cross at Calvary but in the mind of God before we were made. It did not begin to unfold through Jesus's ministry but through centuries of God's guiding hand.

The cross is the culmination of centuries of God's saving work. Because it was revealed time and time again, we can have more assurance that all of God's plans and promises will come to pass.

So, let the cross be a call to not just remember what God has done but to the joy of the Lord, who works everything out in his time and for his glory.

Day 66

Pay your taxes, too, for these same reasons. For government workers need to be paid. They are serving God in what they do. Give to everyone what you owe them: Pay your taxes and government fees to those who collect them, and give respect and honor to those who are in authority.

Romans 13:6-7 (NLT)

"In this world nothing can be said to be certain, except death and taxes."
- Benjamin Franklin (1789 in a letter to Jean-Baptiste Leroy)

In this world, God encourages and even commands us to pay taxes. Why? The world governments, more and more increasingly, are turning their backs on God. Why should we pay money to them? Shouldn't we find every possible way to keep it from them and put it into God's work?

No, it has nothing to do with the government. It has to do with our attitude toward honoring an institution that works at

God's discretion in the first place. Paying taxes has more to do with our witness than the government itself. God calls us to peaceful (1 Thess. 4:11), respectful, and honoring lives (Rom. 13:7).

We are to live lives that people won't be able to bring a complaint against us. Does our tax code give us opportunities to give to God's Kingdom and, therefore, help our own financial situation? Yes, but let us not become corrupt ourselves by choosing to disobey God in this matter. Even paying taxes is an act of worship when done with a heart that desires to honor God.

If you declare with your mouth, "Jesus is Lord," and believe in your heart that God raised him from the dead, you will be saved. For it is with your heart that you believe and are justified, and it is with your mouth that you profess your faith and are saved.

Romans 10:9-10 (NIV)

It doesn't take much to be acceptable to God. It doesn't take hours of meditation. It doesn't take physical pain and suffering on our part. It doesn't take pilgrimages to ancient places. And it doesn't take our good deeds.

To be acceptable by God takes a breath and trust. It takes us using our breath to speak the words "Jesus is Lord." It takes the trust of our belief that he was raised from the dead and will save us from our sins. If we breathe out his words, proclaiming them to this word, and trust in his actions upon the cross and his word, we will be saved.

How simple is the path that God has laid out for us? How monumental is the prize that costs us but our words and our trust? If you have confessed that Jesus is Lord and believe that he had raised Jesus from the dead, you have moved from death to life. Now, live it.

But Christ has indeed been raised from the dead, the firstfruits of those who have fallen asleep. For since death came through a man, the resurrection of the dead comes also through a man. For as in Adam all die, so in Christ all will be made alive.

1 Corinthians 15:20-22 (NIV)

How is it possible for Jesus, who is only one person, to save everyone? That's because it only took one person to tear everything down. Adam is rightly blamed for sin entering into the world because, even though he wasn't the first one to rebel, he was the one who advocated his divine responsibility.

By not protecting his wife, by not stepping into the conversation with the serpent, and by not rejecting the taking of the fruit, Adam rejected God's order of responsibility. He allowed sin to enter into God's perfect creation. Therefore, Jesus, living the life that Adam was created to live and fulfilling the godly requirements of humanity, can now fix what Adam broke.

And because of Jesus' actions on the cross, he was raised from the dead. Anyone who puts their trust in Jesus will likewise be raised to a new life. Death has no victory over those who have placed their trust in Jesus because Jesus conquered death.

"Where, O death, is your victory? Where, O death, is your sting?" The sting of death is sin, and the power of sin is the law. But thanks be to God! He gives us the victory through our Lord Jesus Christ.

1 Corinthians 15:55-57 (NIV)

Victory is a word championed by the Church but seems to take a back seat in the believer's life. We have victory over sin, yet sin still seems to have just as much power now as it did before we put our trust in Jesus. We have victory over death, yet death mortifies us.

We can say we have victory, but do we live it? Do we command the sins in our lives to leave us because they have no power? Do we stand firm in our justification before God, though we feel unworthy? Do we laugh at death and challenge it to come quicker because it has no hold on us? Do we call on God for more trials so that we can have more victory?

If we trust in Jesus, we have victory over everything. Nothing in this world has dominion over us because all authority is Jesus', and we cling to him who has saved us.

Day 70

I give them eternal life, and they will never perish. No one can snatch them away from me, for my Father has given them to me, and he is more powerful than anyone else. No one can snatch them from the Father's hand. The Father and I are one."

John 10:28-30 (NLT)

Ever feel far from God? Ever feel like you've done something so terrible that he no longer wants you? That there is nothing that you can do to fix the relationship and instead just hobble along like a wounded animal licking your emotional, physical, and spiritual wounds?

Just so you know, it's a lie. It's a lie that God doesn't want you. It's a lie that you must live in this world in a broken state. It's a lie that you are too far from God. And it's a lie that you can do nothing to fix it.

Turn and confess. You have sinned; you know it, and God knows it. Hiding it does nothing but prolong the doubt in your mind to fester. It builds the wall ever higher between you and God.

God desires you, not because he needs you or you bring something to the table, but because he created you. He has paid the penalty of sin and brought you into his kingdom, into his family. Confession of sin restores the lines of communication. It doesn't save us; it doesn't make God love us again. It simply acknowledges what both God and we know: we need him.

Nothing can take us out of God's hand, but there are things that can keep us from fully experiencing our relationship with him. Let's eliminate as much of that through confession as we can.

Day 71

For his invisible attributes, namely, his eternal power and divine nature, have been clearly perceived, ever since the creation of the world, in the things that have been made. So they are without excuse.

Romans 1:20 (ESV)

Look at a tree, an insect, a lizard, a hawk, a bush, a rabbit, and a coyote. What do they have in common? They are part of the desert ecosystem. Take one out, and the others suffer. Since I've lived in the desert, I've seen a cycle. One year, there will be an abundance of rabbits and or quail running around. The next, I'll see a lot of coyotes; the following year, there are still a lot of coyotes, but not so many little creatures. Finally, the coyotes are hardly seen in the fourth year, but the quail and rabbits are back in abundance.

As Disney's The Lion King movie would tell us, it's the circle of life. The ecosystem works in harmony, keeping itself in check and providing animals to be eaten and animals who are the eaters. When one is removed from the equation, the others will thrive until their numbers overwhelm the available resources. This is a delicate balance and, in a sense, a symbiotic one. Each creature needs another to keep the ecosystem running smoothly. Yet we are taught so often that each one develops on their own. How? We can see that all facets of the ecosystem need to grow simultaneously so that none overwhelm the environment they're a part of.

This can't be by chance; in fact, the Bible tells us that everything that we see has its beginning in the Creator who created it all.

Look at the world; why are there so many religions? Because we can look around and instantly understand that this world is too complex to be an accident and, therefore, must have a designer. The God of the Bible says that he is the one who created all of it. And it's through his creation that we should take our first steps in seeking him because, as Paul says in Romans 1:20, no one has an excuse because we all have the creation pointing back to its Creator.

Day 72

… for it is written, "As I live, says the Lord, every knee shall bow to me, and every tongue shall confess to God."

Romans 14:11 (ESV)

There are plenty of people who bow their knee to celebrities, politicians, kings, queens, money, drugs, sex, alcohol, gods, nature, themselves, relationships, media, war, and power. But one day, every one of those knees will join the Christian's knee in bowing to Jesus. The difference is that one will be willingly bowed, and the other will be forced to bow. What is your knee bowing to now? Whatever it is will determine how your knee will bow on that day.

To them God has chosen to make known among the Gentiles the glorious riches of this mystery, which is Christ in you, the hope of glory. He is the one we proclaim, admonishing and teaching everyone with all wisdom, so that we may present everyone fully mature in Christ.

Colossians 1:27-28 (NIV)

If you have called on the name of Jesus, accepting him as your Savior, do you realize that you have a mystery within you? A mystery that is both known by you and is being discovered at the same time.

First, we have discovered God, the One we might not even know existed until we encounter him. The God who, once found, is the key that unlocks a greater understanding of ourselves and the world around us.

Once we have made this discovery, we begin to walk with God. Our walk with God is to be a walk of discovery, for if we truly follow a God who lives, then getting to know that God is a journey that will take eternity. The mystery never ends because God's ways are immeasurable.

This is the mystery that we have; Christ lives in us. It is also a mystery to those who do not know him, and it is our responsibility to help reveal God's work in us to them. Are you diving into the mystery that is God? Are you sharing so that others may know him as well?

Therefore he is able to save completely those who come to God through him, because he always lives to intercede for them.

Hebrews 7:25 (NIV)

There are times when we can feel like God can't help us. That an issue we're going through is too great. We think things like, I can't overcome this addiction, or I just keep messing up, and God won't forgive me.

Let's get straight to it: Jesus saves COMPLETELY. That means that every aspect of our lives is saved. From the hair on our heads to the tips of our toes, from the outside of our epidermis to the core of who we are, every aspect is saved. Our thoughts, our chemical makeup, our need for things, and our body's cravings are all under his saving power.

No addiction, mess up, stumble, or action is outside of his saving work. And you have been forgiven. Jesus died and said, "… It is finished … (Jn. 19:30. [NIV])." No more action needs to be taken for you to be saved. All we can do is accept it and seek God's cleansing from all the things that are not of him. And because of his saving work, we can overcome all those things that keep us from fully experiencing him.

So keep going, keep seeking him, and don't give up on him; he hasn't given up on you.

Day 75

For the Son of Man came to seek and to save the lost.

Luke 19:10 (NIV)

Let's be intellectually honest with ourselves for a moment; we can easily get lost. If you have ever been a parent, there are times when you don't know what to do with your kids; you'll feel lost. When starting a new job, even if you studied the field in which you're working, the new experiences can make you feel like you don't know anything at all, and you'll feel lost. Or if you've ever been in a relationship, and you two are trying to decide on a place to eat, but the other person says they don't care, and no matter what you suggest, they don't feel like it, you will feel lost. And when it's late at night, and you're trying to find a street, but there's no street sign to help you out, you'll be lost.

And when calamity comes, and it feels like everything is spiraling out of control, you'll be lost. But there is hope; Jesus is seeking you and desires to save you from your lostness. The calamity is not more enormous than he is. The downward spiral is not deep enough for him not to find you. Jesus is here for you in your lostness; all you have to do is turn to him to be found.

Helping you find a restaurant that's a different story.

Day 76

Have this mind among yourselves, which is yours in Christ Jesus, who, though he was in the form of God, did not count equality with God a thing to be grasped, but emptied himself, by taking the form of a servant, being born in the likeness of men. And being found in human form, he humbled himself by becoming obedient to the point of death, even death on a cross.

                             Philippians 2:5-8 (ESV)

We all know that people can be dumb, mean, and destructive when it comes to dealing with each other. And when people are dumb, mean, and destructive towards us, we get hurt. Then, we give it back to them, justifying our bad behavior by pointing to theirs.

Yet, that's not what Christ has called us to do. Jesus calls us to be like him, being a humble servant who takes the junk of the world and responds with "Father, forgive them, for they do not know what they are doing … (Lk. 23:34, [NIV])."

But do we think we are more significant than Jesus? Do we believe that our responses of hate are a better way than Jesus'? If we do, we need to reexamine what Jesus says because he says no servant is greater than the Master. Those who follow Jesus must realize that he is our Master and that it's his way or the highway.

How do you respond?

"But as for me, I know that my Redeemer lives,

and he will stand upon the earth at last."

Job 19:25 (NLT)

Job didn't know about Jesus. He didn't know that his God and Redeemer would walk on this earth in roughly three thousand years. He didn't know that Jesus would die on the cross. He wouldn't know about the resurrection or the outpouring of the Holy Spirit.

When Job says this, he only knows two things: he's going through hell right now, and God is good.

Why does it seem like you're going through hell in your life? I don't know. Just like Job didn't know, nor did he ever find out why. But I understand why God calls him the most righteous man on earth. It's because Job understood that though the world around us looks to harm us, God will bring us into new life through it. Even though we face the pain and struggles of this life, God is good, and he redeems us.

Job never knew the why of the situation, but he did know who was in control. The question is, do you?

Day 78

Instead, we will speak the truth in love, growing in every way more and more like Christ, who is the head of his body, the church.

Ephesians 4:15 (NLT)

Sticks and stones may break my bones, but words can never hurt me. It's a good chant to say to yourself when people fling insults, but the reality is that the words people say to us can leave lasting marks on our hearts. When someone insults us, belittles us, or berates us, their words can dig themselves into our thoughts and emotions. And at the smallest thing, those words can come back to the surface and flood us with feelings of being inferior and worthlessness.

That's why we are called to speak in love. Truth can be a hard thing for most people to deal with. Especially when that truth shows us we're wrong. And it can feel like an attack. So we, as Jesus' disciples, are to speak this truth with love as the ambassador. It's easy to strike someone down when you're in the right; lifting someone up in the middle of a correction is much more challenging.

Love is to be the motivator, gentleness the moderator, and hope in making the other person greater the end goal.

How would lives change if we first thought of speaking to them in love?

Day 79

This is the confidence we have in approaching God: that if we ask anything according to his will, he hears us. And if we know that he hears us—whatever we ask—we know that we have what we asked of him.

1 John 5:14-15 (NIV)

I may want a good job, a big house, a fat bank account, an easy life, and a loving family. This is what God wants: people to know him through his people loving him and loving others. The two are not necessarily separate, but we tend to desire our wants over those of God's. We'll complain when we don't get what we think God should supply us with when, in reality, we should be seeking to fulfill his desire for us. Only when we have the mindset of doing as God wills do the things we desire become less important. And it's in that place that we will become fulfilled because all we need, we know, to be God himself.

Day 80

Rejoice in our confident hope. Be patient in trouble, and keep on praying.

> Romans 12:12 (NLT)

Do you want to be patient when things are going wrong? Of course not. We want things done now. We want all our problems fixed the moment we ask them to be fixed. Sometimes, we even want them fixed without us asking. And when we don't get them fixed right away, we fall for the serpent's lie that God doesn't care.

Does this catch God off guard? Of course not. That is why he tells us to keep praying and be patient. Pertinence is the ability to take everything that is going on with the understanding that God has a plan. The trouble we face doesn't catch God off guard; rather, he is working through the trouble to bring us into a greater relationship with him.

We might ask ourselves, "But why doesn't God just fix it now?!" God works in our temporal, time-constrained world. Sometimes, things must work themselves out and align so God can work at his maximum.

As God works, we are to rejoice in him, praise him, be patient, and pray. The temporal things of this world will pass, but our relationship with him needs to be deepened and deserves our greatest attention.

Are you experiencing a difficult time that isn't being fixed immediately? I encourage you to keep praying, be patient, and rejoice in God.

His plan is working itself out.

If my people, who are called by my name, will humble themselves and pray and seek my face and turn from their wicked ways, then I will hear from heaven, and I will forgive their sin and will heal their land.

2 Chronicles 7:14 (NIV)

How can God heal our land? What is he calling us to do in order for his divine work to happen?

First, we must humble ourselves. We must stop trying to be the ones who need all the credit, the limelight, and the accolades of the world. Until we do, why should we call on God to heal our land?

Second, we are to pray. We need to steep ourselves in prayer, praying on our own throughout our daily lives and praying with our brothers and sisters in the Lord. Until we do, why should we call for God to heal our land?

Third, we are to seek God's face. We need to be holy people who seek to be worthy to be in the presence of the Living God. We are to be conformed by the Spirit to the likeness of the Son. Until we do, why should we call for God to heal our land?

Finally, we are to turn away from our wicked ways. We need to stop playing with sin, condemning it first in our own lives, leaving it in the grave, and relying on the Holy Spirit living in us to squash it when it tries to come back into our lives. Until we do, why should we call for God to heal our land?

God desires to help our land, but until we want to follow him in the way he calls us to, why should we expect him to heal that which we do not truly desire to be fixed?

Don't worry about anything; instead, pray about everything. Tell God what you need, and thank him for all he has done. Then you will experience God's peace, which exceeds anything we can understand. His peace will guard your hearts and minds as you live in Christ Jesus.

Philippians 4:6-7 (NLT)

Peace and prayer go hand in hand. Why are we not experiencing the peace that Jesus talks about in John 14:27? Why are we not experiencing peace that passes understanding? Because that kind of peace is cultivated in a prayerful relationship with God.

Prayer is the pillar of our relationship with God, teaching us dependence, authenticity, and grace.

Being in God's word is good. It grows our understanding of who God is and gives us reason to trust in his promises. But when it is not coupled with a prayerful life, a life where our first thought is to communicate with God, we lose our vibrant access with the Living God.

And when that access is lost, our faith becomes stale and legalistic.

Today, do not pray in your ordinary manner. Instead, talk with God as if you are catching your best friend up on what is going on in your life. And allow the access to the Creator of the Universe to come alive.

Day 83

Confess your sins to each other and pray for each other so that you may be healed. The earnest prayer of a righteous person has great power and produces wonderful results.

> James 5:16 (NLT)

Confession of sins brings healing—healing of the body, healing of the spirit, healing of the emotions, healing of the mind, and healing of relationships.

I recently heard a pastor tell a story about his father. His father was an elder in a church somewhere in the mid-west United States. Even though he was an elder in the church, he didn't get along with the pastor. They had two very different approaches on how to run the church and came into conflict often. One day, the doctors found cancer in the father's body and told him he needed surgery. While he was in the hospital awaiting the surgery, the pastor reluctantly came to see him.

The doctor later told the family what happened after the pastor arrived. The father confessed to the pastor that he had sinned against him and asked for forgiveness because he wanted to make it right. The pastor left without giving forgiveness and mending the relationship. When the father went into surgery, the doctor said the black spot had dissolved, and the father was healed.

So often we live in pain, spiritually, mentally, physically, emotionally, and relationally because we do not confess that we have hurt people and are in need of forgiveness. As a first step of healing, we may need to confess our sins to each other. In doing so, maybe we can begin to experience God's healing for our lives.

Do you have anything that needs confession?

Day 84

Rejoice always, pray without ceasing, give thanks in all circumstances; for this is the will of God in Christ Jesus for you.

                              1 Thessalonians 5:16-18 (ESV)

What is the will of God? Simple: rejoice in good times and bad. Pray, not just in times of trouble. Give thanks when it seems like there is nothing to be thankful about. That is the will of God that we get our eyes off ourselves and onto him.

For the grace of God has appeared that offers salvation to all people. It teaches us to say "No" to ungodliness and worldly passions, and to live self-controlled, upright and godly lives in this present age…

Titus 2:11-12 (NIV)

How does grace teach us to say "no?" Doesn't it teach us compassion so that our anger does not burn against others, just as God's anger doesn't burn against us through Jesus? Doesn't it teach us forgiveness so we can forgive the deepest of wounds, just as God has forgiven our rebellious acts through Jesus? Doesn't it teach us to love others even at their worst, just as God forgave us through Jesus, even while we were still in sin? And doesn't grace teach us to desire to obey God with our lives, abstaining from the sinful desires within us, just as Jesus showed what was possible through the power of the Holy Spirit?

God's grace should be an instructor to our lives so that we learn to love, forgive, and obey as God has shown us. Grace that has been poured out on us should, in turn, be poured out to those around us. Today, are you allowing grace to teach and instruct you how to live out your faith?

Day 86

If another believer sins against you, go privately and point out the offense. If the other person listens and confesses it, you have won that person back.

Matthew 18:15 (NLT)

The primary thrust of the Gospel is restoring relationships. Through the cross, Jesus opened the way for the restoration of the relationship between God and man and between men and women.

Too often, instead of seeking restoration in our relationships, we allow debatable or secondary theology to divide the very relationships that Jesus wants to restore. Most denominations in the Church have risen up because of disagreements in theology that have nothing to do with the core of the Gospel.

Are there unmovable truths that cannot be compromised? Yes. But are there also opinions that, from an eternal perspective, do not matter? Yes.

One of a Christian's primary jobs is to connect people with God. Our second job is as important as the first, and that is to restore our relationships with others.

I pray that we will see past our own thoughts on theological doctrines and instead desire that the body of the Savior, Christ Jesus our Lord, be built up and not torn apart. Are you building up or tearing down today?

Instead, be kind to each other, tenderhearted, forgiving one another, just as God through Christ has forgiven you.

Ephesians 4:32 (NLT)

Every action we take must be with the mindset of what God has done for us through the person of Jesus. Every word we say to someone, every action we engage in, and every thought that passes our mind needs to be joined with the reality of what God has done for us.

Therefore, can we gossip? No, Christ saved us from it. Can we harbor anger? No, Christ saved us from it. Can we hold back forgiveness toward someone? No, Christ forgave us. Can we belittle others? No, Christ came for all.

When we do the things that Christ saved us from, no matter what the end goal is, we have sinned and need repentance and forgiveness. Let us live our lives with joy and an understanding of what God has done for us. Let us let it penetrate every aspect of our lives until there is nothing left in them except only the praise of God and our pointing back to him.

Day 88

Who can find a virtuous and capable wife? She is more precious than rubies … She carefully watches everything in her household and suffers nothing from laziness. Her children stand and bless her. Her husband praises her …

Proverbs 31:10, 27-28 (NLT)

God made man and saw that without a woman, there would be no perfection in this world. Man and woman together complete God's creation. A wife is a helpmate to accomplish all that God has set before the family. She is the compassionate refuge for her child and a reprieve from the harsh world for her husband.

Every man should seek out a wife who is too godly for them because it will challenge him to follow God more closely. And every woman should seek to be too godly for any man so that she will find one that follows God.

Once a man finds a godly woman, they should treasure her beyond anything they could ever earn. And once a woman finds a godly man, encourage him to carry on through this life's hardships. When both husband and wife delight and treasure each other, they will discover that God delights in their union.

Charm is deceptive, and beauty does not last; but a woman who fears the Lord will be greatly praised.

Proverbs 31:30 (NLT)

The physical things are easy: makeup, new clothes, workouts, hairdressers, hair replacement, liposuction, stomach stapling, plastic surgery. If you have the money or a way to pay for something, you can keep yourself looking good for a long time.

On the other hand, internal things are hard. You have to develop compassion for those who hurt you, hold your tongue when everything in you wants to scream, respect those who disrespect you, live a generous life when that means you have to live with less and build people up by looking for what's best for them.

Our society is all about the physical, which is the me mentality. God is all about the internal, which is the them mentality. One sets its eyes on the path of death, while the other plants its roots in the stream of eternal life.

Which are you doing today?

Day 90

Oh, the depth of the riches of the wisdom and knowledge of God! How unsearchable his judgments, and his paths beyond tracing out!

Romans 11:33 (NIV)

I once had someone tell me that they already knew everything about God and that they no longer needed to read the Bible.

So, the finite mind of a human is in a constant state of learning and experiencing new things. Who has only about 80 years of life to experience everything in this world? Who, as a human race, is still discovering new things about the world we live in? Has that human learned all there is to know about God?

Let's be clear: If God is really the infinite Creator of all that there is in the universe, then no created being can hope to fully comprehend that God. When I return to the Bible and read it, I learn new things about God and about myself.

Do not ever believe that you know everything there is to know about God; once you believe that, you will show how little you actually know.

So, as you end this devotional, this is a charge to you. Keep growing. Never stop!

Afterword

Dear Reader,

I want to thank you for spending the last 90 days with me. I pray this has led to a deepening of your faith and that you have experienced God's holy life in new ways. God bless you as you continue to grow, and if I don't see you in this life, I'll see you in eternity to come.

In Christ's Grip,

Jeremiah

Made in the USA
Middletown, DE
03 February 2025